The Art of Social-Network Marketing

Ken Powers

Tacoma, Washington

2011

The Art of Social-Network Marketing

Editor: Charles K. Powers
Cover Design: Ken Powers

Copyright © 2011 by Ken Powers
http://www.powersfineart.com/

ALL RIGHTS RESERVED.

This book contains material protected under International and Federal Copyright Laws and Treaties. Any unauthorized reprint or use of this material is prohibited. No part of this book may be reproduced or transmitted in any form or by any means, electronic or mechanical, including photocopying, recording, or by any information storage and retrieval system without express written permission from the author / publisher.

Inquires should be addressed to:

Ken Powers
4525 Tacoma Avenue South
Tacoma, Washington 98418

ISBN 978-1-257-95990-7

Powers Fine Art Publishing

The Art of Social-Network Marketing

Table of Contents

Introduction..9
Strategy...13
   The Network-Marketing Strategy........................15
The Virtual Storefront...19
   Establishing a Web Presence...............................21
Search Engine Optimization (SEO)...............................25
   Content and Search Rankings..............................27
   Link Exchange...31
   Interlinking & Anchor Text....................................33
   Encouraging Social Sharing.................................37
Social Networking Overview..39
   Demographic Motivation.......................................41
   Successful Interaction..43
   Time Management...45
Twitter..47
   What is Twitter?..49
   Developing A Follower-Base.................................53
   Twitter Lists...55
   Hash-tags..57
   #FollowFriday...59
   Follower Limits...63
   Composing Posts/Tweets....................................65
Facebook..69
   What is Facebook?...71
   Facebook Marketing Methods..............................73
   The Profile..75

- The Business Page..79
- Business Page Marketing.......................................81
- Custom Tabs & Landing Pages..............................83
- Your Page's Profile Picture....................................85
- Provide Great Content..89
- Use Facebook as Page..95
- Use of the "@" Symbol..97
- Product Specific Content.......................................99
- Facebook Ads...101

Google+..103
- Why Use Google+?..105
- The Google+ Profile..107
- Circles and Posts..109
- Presentation of Media..111

YouTube..113
- What is YouTube?..115

LinkedIn...119
- Why Utilize LinkedIn?..121

StumbleUpon...123
- What is StumbleUpon?..125
- Increasing StumbleUpon Traffic.........................127
- Su.pr Link Shortener...131

Account Security..133
- Help, I've Been Hacked!.....................................135

Conclusion..137
- Final Remarks and Insights.................................139

Index..141
- Alphabetical Index..143
- About the Author..146

Introduction

Whether it is a painting, a musical recording, or a revolutionary new product with global improvement potential, the personal decision to begin self-marketing via an Internet-based approach can be very exciting. The uninitiated often enter into this experience expecting instantaneous results. Quite frequently they are met with a disappointing customer-base, lackluster sales, and an immeasurable loss of invested time. Because of this, they fail to see the relevance of this modern marketing method and eventually abandon their efforts.

I have received many e-mails from individuals who are frustrated, lost, disappointed, and depressed simply because they are trying to use Internet marketing tools in an ineffective manner and ultimately determine the endeavor is a waste of valuable time. Correspondents request information explaining how I am successfully utilizing Internet marketing tools in order to sell my artwork.

There is a myriad of conflicting data available concerning how to utilize the Internet for marketing and it is often difficult to decipher. The information that exists, is spread across multiple web sites, PDF documents, forums, blogs, newsletters, and within services that require substantial payment to aid in your quest. I have spent hundreds of hours researching and putting into practice many of the tips that I have found to be the most logical and have experimented with them in order to determine their effectiveness. I have combined and utilized the most effective across multiple social-networking services and have essentially created a cohesive marketing system for the promotion and sale of my artwork. Because of the elusive nature of many of these tips, I felt there was a great need to have a resource that combines this information into a single volume.

I undertook the writing of this book because I have been in the position of the complete disbeliever. In fact, I had actually made several failed attempts at using various social-networking services before I began to find techniques that made them effective for me. I completely understand the frustrations that manifest themselves simply due to not knowing how to properly approach these modern marketing tools.

When I began to analyze the techniques I found to be most useful, I realized that not all social-networking services could be utilized in exactly the same way and it is this information I wish to present to the reader. I want you to walk away from this text understanding techniques to effectively utilize each of the most popular social-networking services in conjunction with a cohesive centralized marketing philosophy which can help aid in increased sales.

This book is not meant to be a complete step-by-step instruction manual but instead is a collection of concepts and tips that can be combined and utilized in many different ways individual to one's specific purpose, products, or services.

Realize in advance that there is no marketing magic wand to be waved and in order to become successful it requires an investment of time and effort forging relationships. I have included information and techniques for some of the top social-networking services that are most effective for marketing and I sincerely hope this information will aid the reader of this text in a successful online marketing experience. Although different methods may be required in order to successfully market through any given social community, there is a basic foundation that applies to them all and if you desire to use more than just the services I am going to present to you, you will still have a toolbox of effective techniques. The key to success is to enter into this endeavor with a plan and a clear marketing strategy.

Strategy

The Network-Marketing Strategy

An effective marketing strategy begins with a very basic premise: *"People don't purchase products they don't know exist."* Quite simply, this means that it is necessary for as many people as possible to see our products or services if we plan to be successful selling them. Logically, the greater the number of people that see what we are selling, the greater the chance we will have to sell our wares. Obviously, if we believe the above premise to be true, we need to discover and implement ways in which to get our products in front of the eyes of as many people as possible. In this modern age, what better way to reach an enormous potential customer-base than by using the Internet and social-networking?

According to Edison Research, as of 2010, 84% of our population has access to the Internet from some location. Additionally, 6 in 7 homes with Internet connections, have broadband and 6 in 10 homes with Internet connections have a Wi-Fi network. It is a large segment of our population that currently has daily access to the Internet and these numbers are continuing to grow.

As the years have passed, Internet social-networking has continued to see an explosive amount of growth. Edison Research reports that as of June 2011, 52% of Americans over the age of 12 have a personal profile page on Facebook, MySpace, LinkedIn or one of several other social-networking web sites. As of this writing, Facebook has reached over 600 million users while Twitter usage has hit the 17 million user mark in the United States and an estimated 100 million users worldwide. Approximately 46 million Americans over the age of 12 check their social media sites several times a day.

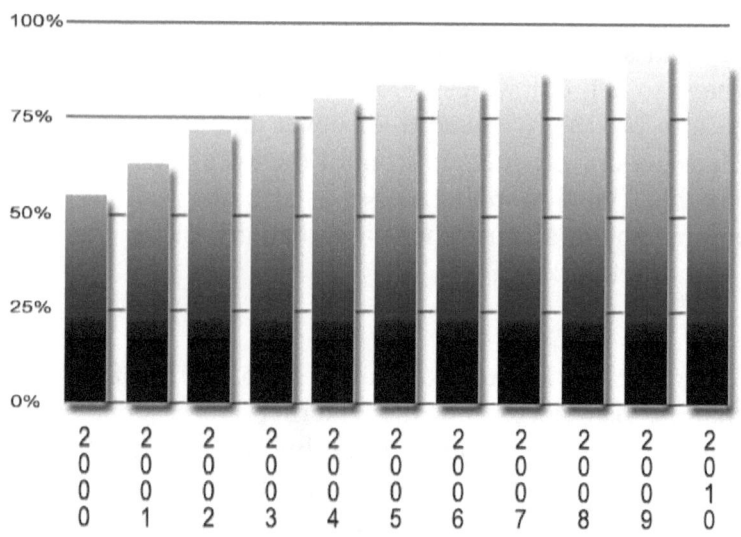

Traditionally, product purchasing recommendations from family and friends have been the most trusted. According to Cone Inc., however, 81% of US consumers now go online to do additional research, with 55% looking for user reviews, and

10% soliciting advice from their social network groups. ExactTarget's research also indicates that 90% of people trust the recommendations of their Facebook friends while Edison Research claims that 31% of daily Twitter users ask their followers for product opinions.

With the increasing level of Internet, social-networking, and e-commerce utilization, it is only logical that one should investigate marketing through this easily accessible channel. It allows you to promote your business while receiving immediate feedback from potential customers. Spending an hour a day posting messages and comments of interest to your target audience opens a line of communication that allows you to learn about your customers and to connect with them in real time. I utilize Facebook, Twitter, StumbleUpon, MySpace, YouTube, and a personal web site to reach as many people as possible in order to promote my original paintings and prints. Each of these services provides an avenue with which to present information to potential clients. Although similar in concept, however, each operates in a unique fashion and combining them into an effective centralized marketing strategy can be confusing and mysterious to first-time users. It is easy to become discouraged when the myriad of Internet-based potential purchasers fail to flock to a carefully designed page.

While it is tempting to simply create profiles on every social-networking site in existence, haphazardly proceeding without having a preconceived marketing plan can end in frustrating disappointment. I have found through extensive experimentation that it is much more effective to create a central base of operations to which all other web-presences point. This essentially creates a marketing network which is designed to attract potential customers and to drive them to a central storefront from which they can purchase products or services. For example, I have a personal web site at http://www.powersfineart.com designed to directly sell my fine art prints and original paintings. It contains my biography and artist statement as well as additional information about my art and portfolio books. I utilize Twitter and Facebook to direct traffic to my main site and StumbleUpon to notify people of new paintings as they become available. The key to making this strategy effective, however, is to have a follower-base established in each of the social-networks.

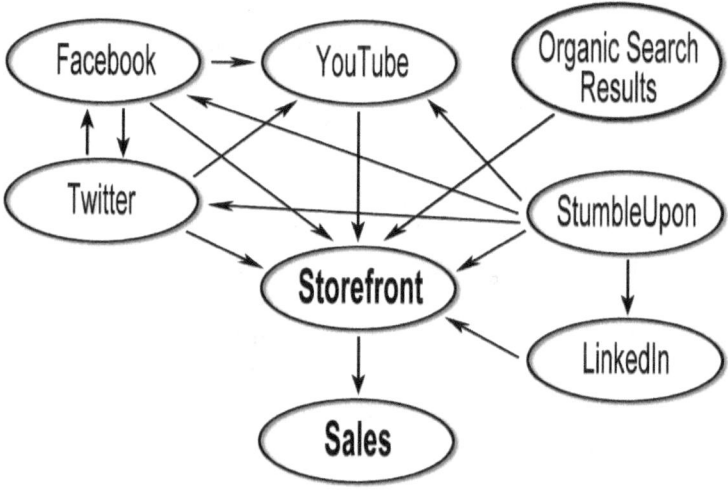

The following sections of this book are designed to help establish some clear marketing methods and tips designed to aid in gaining followers in these main social-networking services as well as how to use the services to drive traffic to the main hub of your centralized Internet-based marketing program.

The Virtual Storefront

Establishing a Web Presence

Creating a central location to display and sell products or services is an important Internet-based marketing strategy. This site is the virtual face of your company on the Internet and must exude a professional demeanor designed to encourage potential customers to purchase. Initially putting your best foot forward can mean the difference between developing a client base or losing potential clientele. Often, one only has a single opportunity to make a lasting impression and this first impression is the key to selling products. Establishing an air of professionalism increases a purchaser's confidence level and demonstrating to clients that it is completely safe to purchase through your web site by appearing trustworthy can only lead to future success.

The virtual storefront needs to be easily navigable and provide answers to questions and access to product information with a minimal number of mouse clicks and unnecessary pages. As visitors navigate through the site, they should be motivated to learn more about your products and services. Potential customers who see a very haphazardly designed web site will more than likely move along to another where they feel more comfortable. As an Internet product purchaser myself, I have experienced this many times. If I have the choice between purchasing a product through a very amateurish web site or one that has a professional trustworthy appearance, I am purchasing through the latter. Take some time and make sure your storefront looks like a place where someone would want to shop. In this age of identity theft and economically motivated purchasing apprehension, a professional appearance means everything. The Internet-based storefront is the core of your product's web presence so devote quality time to its construction.

This central location is the web site to which you will be driving traffic from all other sources. Whether it is a hard-coded HTML page posted on rented server space, a web site provided by Wicz, an Etsy or Ebay storefront, or something similar provided by many other services on the Internet, without this centralized location the entrepreneur needs to continually post product information and photos to every social-networking site to which he or she belongs. I like to compare this to repeatedly going door to door, demonstrating your products to every neighborhood in the world. Updating all your web presences has the potential of consuming many hours of precious time. It is much simpler to post links back to this central storefront where most of your product data and photos exist.

In addition to simply being a lot of extra work, continually posting the same information to multiple social-networking sites fails to accomplish a very important traffic generating task. By posting links back to your central node from all other web presences instead of simply repeatedly posting the same data, the central node's ranking in major web search engine results is increased. The more links existing that direct traffic back to your virtual storefront, the higher the page will rank in most major search engines. This simple philosophy is part of creating a Search Engine Optimization strategy or SEO. By supplying links back to a main web site/storefront, one not only informs potential customers of product information, but also increases the level at which the main site appears during a generalized web search which ultimately generates more organic search traffic and therefore more potential purchasing customers.

Search Engine Optimization (SEO)

Content and Search Rankings

It would be extremely negligent not to stress the importance of taking steps to improve your virtual storefront's search engine ranking. There is an entire industry developed to the art of Search Engine Optimization (SEO) and it is not unusual for large companies to employ specialists in this particular field. Major corporations see the benefit of addressing this issue and so should you. Although these corporations are additionally spending a lot of money to purchase better spots in major search engine results, they are also incorporating some basic techniques as well. These are the methods that can, and should, be used by all individuals who are marketing via the Internet.

Beginning with properly coded web pages can lead to a much stronger web presence. If you are coding your own web site, make sure you have correctly entered the page's meta-tag and keyword data. This is critical information in the HTML code that helps search engines determine the content that exists on your pages and it is amazing how often novices exclude it.

Ensure that each page of the site has a unique title. The title appears at the top of the browser window or in a browser's tabs and is also one of the first things a search engine examines. Since the title should demonstrate what content is on a particular page of a web site, it is one of the key elements used to index your pages. When one performs a keyword search through a search engine, this title is displayed in the results as well as the contents of another HTML element known as a meta-description.

This brief description of the web site is also included in the HTML code of the page and needs to be short so the search engine can properly categorize the page but also needs to be interesting enough to encourage people to click the search engine's link to see your products or services. The page title and description are prominently displayed in a search engine's results and therefore should not be ignored. Since these elements help describe what a page contains, care must be taken to ensure that the content of the page is descriptive and useful.

One of the simplest steps you can take to improve SEO, beyond having correctly formed HTML pages, is to include textual content on your pages. I often see web sites that simply have images of products, paintings, or sculptures with no other information. Simple images don't provide data to search engine page crawlers. It is important to have descriptive textual information on the site that clearly indicates what the images represent. The content should be relevant to the product and customers should be able to effortlessly find answers to their questions. By having informative text, search engines such as Google, Yahoo, and Bing know where to place your site when a web user specifies search criteria. As a painter promoting my watercolor artwork, my main web site at http://www.powersfineart.com/ includes my biography, artist statement, a main page describing who I am and what I do as well as gallery pages with instant purchasing options and pages which refer to my portfolio book. Each page of the web site contains a section of text which clearly describes what is in that particular area and this text is crawled by the search engine spiders to help aid in categorizing the site. Providing this information as actual text and not a graphical representation of text helps insure these results. Content is one of the most important elements to utilize in an effort to create a high-ranking web site.

Many search engines offer tools to aid you in making sure your site conforms to these qualifications and Google is no exception. The Google webmaster tools page found at https://www.google.com/webmasters/tools/home allows you to submit your web site's URL and, if desired, an associated sitemap.xml file. The sitemap.xml file, which is used by multiple search engine services, can be useful in letting search engines know about pages on your web site which might not be very easily discovered. There are many utilities on the Internet which can help generate this file and although it isn't required, it can help if your page has dynamically created content or the pages on your web site are not well linked. Additionally, the Google webmaster tools page can be used to diagnose your web site in order to make suggested changes that might increase it's search ranking. This is a valuable tool to consider using and can improve your web site's visibility.

Link Exchange

Earlier when I spoke of the importance of having a main web site or storefront to draw traffic, I also mentioned how linking back to this page from other sites can increase the search engine ranking of your web site. One often overlooked but very useful way to do this in addition to implementing social-networking sites, is to arrange with other web site owners to exchange links. Many web site owners, including myself, have a page dedicated to sharing links to friends or acquaintances who have similar products or interests within my industry. By placing a link to another individual's web site on your own, you are increasing their web presence and search engine ranking. By mutually agreeing to perform this act with another site owner, both individuals can benefit. Increasing link traffic to your site is one of the most effective ways to help garner more visitation and to increase search engine discoverability. All it takes is a bit of networking in order to find other site owners within your industry who are willing to reciprocate. I have links on my web site to several artists whose work I admire and we have mutually enjoyed the effects of this relationship. If you are able to exchange links with a very high traffic site, the benefits can be even more pronounced.

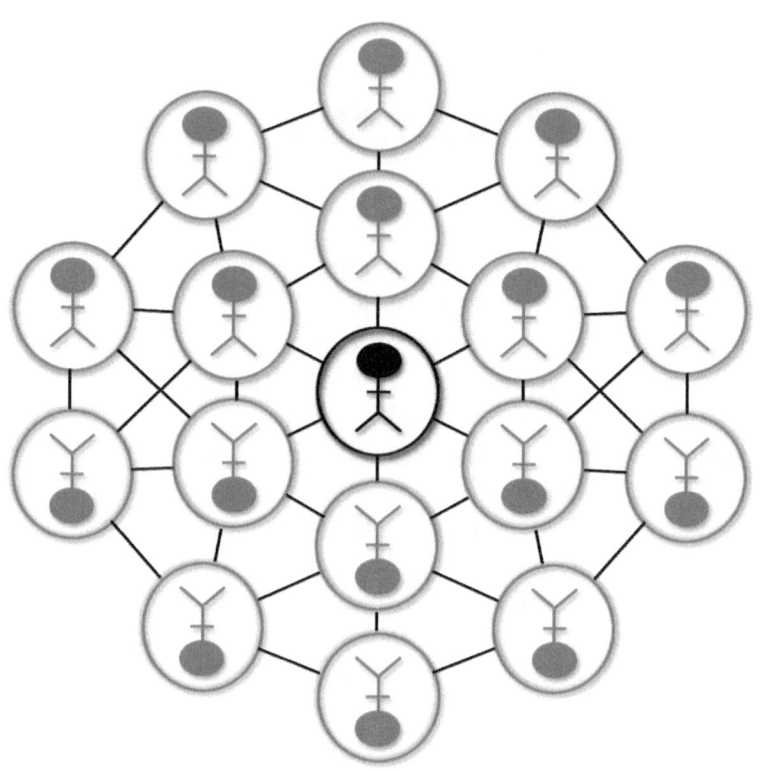

Interlinking & Anchor Text

When we spoke earlier about the importance of having "inbound links" to a website in order to increase search engine discoverability as well as boosting organic visitation, we also mentioned creating "outbound links" to sites of fellow industry professionals. Outbound links can help entice "link exchange" participation from other individuals. However, one might not realize there is another type of linking that can aid in search engine discoverability, visitation, and ranking.

The third, and most often overlooked, linking method is known as "interlinking" which is a form "deep linking." The desired effect of "deep linking" within a web site is to build up back links to one's home page in order to increase it's presence within search results. The "interlinking" form of "deep linking" is used to connect relevant information on one's website through the use of links within its textual content. The goal of this type of search engine optimization is to increase the authority of an entire web site and not just its home page. If you look at many of the page content descriptions within my artist promotion website at http://www.powersfineart.com/, you will find there are links within the text that connect to my contact page, print shop, or other relevant areas. Besides having simple menu navigation, there are links within each page's text that direct the user to other areas of the site as well. Experts who focus upon search engine optimization (SEO), often state that web content developers should have one "interlink" for every couple hundred words of text. The reason this is helpful, is when a website is crawled by the search engines in order to determine content and ranking, the crawlers follow the "interlinks" which count as additional connections to individual pages within a site. Each page, therefore, gets another small boost in search engine ranking by utilizing this method.

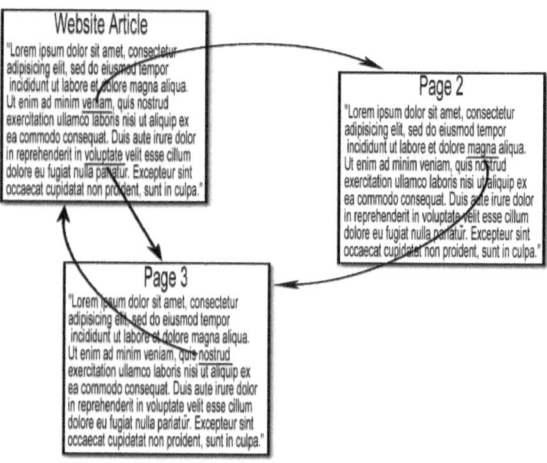

The text that is displayed which describes the "interlinks" is another important factor to consider. Not only does this link point to other relevant information on your site, it also tells what content can be found at that location. By using explanatory descriptors, or "anchor text," for your hyperlinks, you are further enforcing the search engine's knowledge of each page's content. By ensuring that the links are relevant to the content of your page, you also help reinforce the search engine's subject matter determinations which can aid in properly placing your site in search results.

Encouraging Social Sharing

2011 has proven to be a very interesting year for social-network marketing and one of the most incredible advancements involves the king of all search engines, Google. The company holds a 65% market share according to *Experian Hitwise* and earlier in the year they made some bold changes that all network marketers need to know. Google modified their search algorithms which determine the type of online information that is most relevant and they have specifically chosen to place greater emphasis upon original social content. Socially shared content now bubbles to the top of the search engine's results. In other words, for the online marketer, one not only needs to create high-quality content, but also needs to actively encourage its sharing throughout social media.

There are some key steps to be taken to ensure these new algorithms place your virtual storefront near the top of search results. The first is to create quality content that is unique. Posting the same information that is available everywhere else on the web will not aid your quest. However, posting content that is original and has a unique perspective can encourage high rankings.

The second step is to create a Google profile and make sure it is updated with all your current information. This includes links to your main website as well as Twitter and Facebook Pages. When someone searches Google for your name, your profile will be the first thing to appear in the results and it is accompanied by links to your important marketing sites. Additionally, the Google profile is required in order to begin utilizing Google's +1 feature.

Google's +1 button is the company's answer to Facebook's "Like." User's can click the button to essentially vote for the relevance of a particular site, page, newsletter, or article. Google has publicly stated that this button directly influences the placement of pages within its search results. This announcement alone should be motivation to utilize a Google Profile for self-promotion of pages and products, and should stress the importance of including the +1 button on all storefront pages in order to encourage sharing and, ultimately, search engine optimization.

If you think Google is the only search provider headed in this direction, you would be mistaken. Bing has also begun increasingly favoring social content in their search results. In fact, the search engine has also integrated Facebook sharing features as encouragement. Users can now easily share information and images they find through Bing to their Facebook friends.

With an increasing tendency for major search engines to favor socially shared content in their search results, this only reinforces the need to incorporate social-networking into one's Internet marketing strategy.

Social Networking Overview

Demographic Motivation

It is easy to discount social-networking's marketing viability based upon its perceived usage as a tool to merely keep in touch with family and friends. However, if we look more deeply, we can see that we can substantiate it's viability by merely looking at the sheer number of people who utilize it. If we return to our original marketing premise based around maximum product visibility, discounting social media marketing would be a huge mistake. With Facebook topping 600 million users and Twitter topping 100 million users, there is a huge possible consumer base that exists within this medium.

Many of these services use demographically served ads to subsist and because of this, the services have already determined the interests of their user base. When people enroll in a social-network community, they often supply information that indicates their interests and hobbies. The services also make suggestions to users in the community as to who to follow based upon similar interests. Building micro-communities of like-minded individuals is the key to demographically based product promotion and the work has already been done in this regard. There are many tools that exist within individual social-networks to help aid one in getting product or service information in front of the right eyes and once you become involved in promoting products in this manner, you will be amazed at the framework that exists specifically for this purpose.

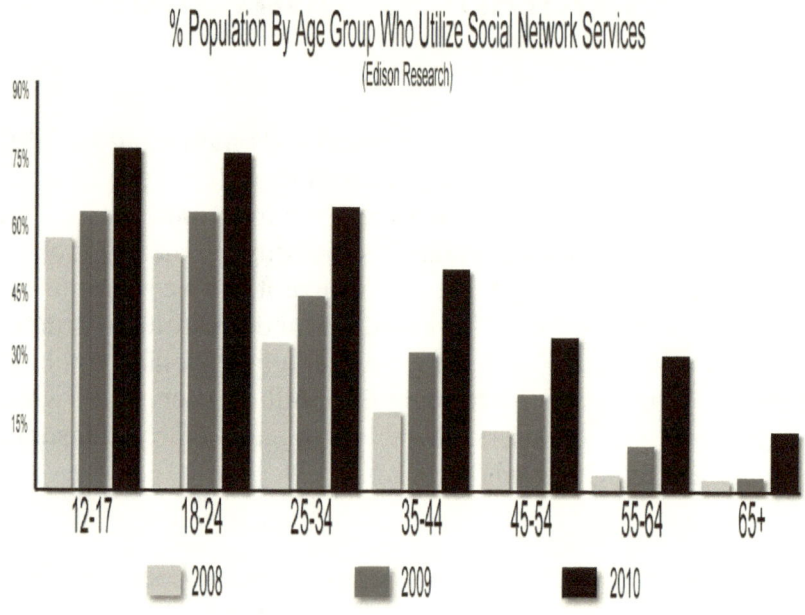

Social-network product promotion can be an extremely satisfying experience if approached in the appropriate manner. Because these networks are based nearly entirely around social communication and interaction, however, there are some simple common-sense concepts that can really aid one in their social-media success.

Successful Interaction

Utilizing social media over the course of the past 28 years in one form or another has taught me several valuable techniques which have become very useful. Whether it was through a dial-up bulletin-board system, posting in a newsgroup, utilizing forums, or modern use of Twitter and Facebook, there are some simple concepts and common-sense rules of etiquette that apply to them all.

In order to create a successful network of relationships, Internet marketers need to realize there are absolutely no shortcuts. Time and effort must be invested in establishing connections. This means communicating, sharing, contributing, and generally participating in conversations. Over time, this investment will reward itself with success. Portraying oneself as being helpful and courteous can go a long way toward building essential long-term social-network relationships. It is important to realize that in addition to building strong friendships, every status update and social-network post is also magnifying one's presence in organic search results and it is best if these show up in a positive light.

As with any endeavor that involves human interaction, it is imperative to realize that common societal rules apply. One must be polite, thank fellow users for their efforts that aid you, and avoid being rude or condescending. It is amazing what lending a helping hand and addressing individuals by their names in a friendly manner can accomplish. There are always those who utilize these services who just don't seem to understand that taking a combative polarizing stance on posted topics does nothing constructive, fosters disdain, and is counter-productive to creating solid relationships.

Social media is about conversation and collaborative efforts. Realize in advance that building networked relationships is the key to successful usage of any social environment. Engaging content and presentation of useful information is the key to keeping people returning to your online presence.

Since one is going to be utilizing multiple social-network services in their marketing endeavor, it should be noted that it can be very useful to realize that even if you are only just beginning the social-network marketing journey, you are still promoting yourself and products. Because of this, it is logical to maintain a consistent presence, or "brand," across all services. Utilizing the same icon/avatar and user name across multiple social-networks makes it much simpler to find your business. You are essentially attempting to establish a consistently owned identity across the entire World Wide Web.

Time Management

Believe it or not, a social-networker could spend literally hours per day attempting to update followers and fans through social-media once a followership begins to develop. If you allow it, social-networking can consume all the time you would normally dedicate to product refinement, creative processes, and other avenues of promotion. It is important to establish some time-limits and restrictions in order to keep social-networking from becoming overwhelming.

I recommend allotting a specific amount of time per day to be utilized for social-network promotion. Spending too much time seems to result in diminished returns and can also lead to over-posting, clogging follower news feeds, and generating a negative web presence which can lead to loss of members of your fan base. An hour or so should be an adequate amount of time to post new content, comment on the post's of others, and maintain a visible and effective web-presence.

Developing a social-network marketing work-flow that is effective for you is a very individual matter. However, I prefer to check Facebook Fan Page interactions first, Profile second, Twitter news-feed third, and finally e-mail. Adhering to this simple schedule allows me to quickly move through the important processes of the day and further allows me to effectively utilize the very small amount of marketing time available to me. Developing a quick and efficient work-flow is the key to effectively utilizing modern marketing tools such as social-media without it becoming an aggravating and unnecessary consumption of time.

Because there are literally hundreds of social-networks from which to stage a marketing campaign, product or service promoters need to find communities which cater to the particular goods or services they are marketing. My time is most effectively utilized by focusing upon just a couple social-networks instead of trying to maintain a presence in every community. The following sections of this book will focus upon specific networks and the methods and tips which I have found to yield optimal results.

Twitter

What is Twitter?

Twitter defines itself as, *"a real-time information network that connects you to the latest information about what you find interesting."*

Fundamentally, Twitter is composed of 140 character bursts of information that may contain headlines, photos, or videos. Users follow other members of the community and each person can use Twitter to tell stories, update people about their lives, or even sell products. Edison Research reports that the majority of Twitter users are actually "lurkers" who never post to the service but merely follow the Tweets of others. They further report that 70% of regular Twitter users post status updates to at least one social-networking service such as Facebook. Twitter is functioning more as a news service compared to Facebook and many other social-networking sites and that is the way they wish to publicly portray themselves.

According to the Twitter web site, *"Twitter connects businesses to customers in real-time. Businesses use Twitter to quickly share information with people interested in their products and services, gather real-time market intelligence and feedback, and build relationships with customers, partners and influential people. From brand lift, to CRM, to direct sales,*

Twitter offers businesses a chance to reach an engaged audience."

Incredibly, in 2011, Edison Research reported that 8% of Americans over the age of 12 use Twitter. That equates to approximately 17 million people just in the United States alone. Although Twitter is based in San Francisco, it reaches users on a global scale and there are an estimated 100 million users world wide.

Edison Research's data also indicates that, *"The percentage of Twitter users who follow brands is more than three times higher than similar behavior expressed by social-networking users in general. Significant percentages of regular Twitter users report using the service not only to seek opinions about companies, products and services, but to provide those opinions as well."*

The research data indicates that Twitter is a perfect vehicle for delivering news and information concerning products and promotions to a large and continually growing segment of our population. In fact, Apple and Twitter have recently entered into an agreement to deeply integrate Twitter into Apple's mobile operating system beginning with iOS5 in the Fall of 2011.

Online influence can translate into real world transactions and creating a network of relationships with current and potential customers can lead to rewarding results. By building and nurturing this network, marketers can create relationships with people who will get to know them, trust them and will ultimately conduct business with them. In order to accomplish this, however, social-network marketers need to invest time toward establishing a follower-base within Twitter's social community.

Developing A Follower-Base

Using Twitter to reach thousands of people with product promotions, etc... requires that people are actually following your business through the service. Being followed doesn't just confirm an existing affinity, it increases purchasing intent and the willingness to recommend your product or services to others.

Beginning to use Twitter is as simple as joining, choosing a user name, and creating a free account. Building a loyal follower-base, however, can take some time and patience. There are several steps you can take to help speed this process along, however.

When you create your account, pick a user name that people can clearly associate with you and your product. If you are using a consistent brand across multiple social media platforms, you might stick with that. I try to use "Powers Fine Art" for all my network presences but if you are promoting yourself as an artist, it might be better to just use your name since it makes it easier for people to find you. Put some thought into this since it is difficult to switch to a different user name after you have established a loyal following within the community. In my case, my Twitter user name is Powers_Fine_Art so the URL of my Twitter page is http://www.twitter.com/powers_fine_art.

Every Twitter account can display a profile image, a brief 140 character biography, and a web site link. Be sure to use a professional image for the profile picture. This will be the first thing people see before they observe your posts and first impressions are everlasting. Just leaving the profile image blank is sure to dissuade people from following you. Bear in mind that this image doesn't necessarily have to be a head shot. It could also be a sample of your product or something similar.

Additionally, Twitter allows 160 characters to create a clear and concise biography that explains who you are and what you do. For some reason they allow 20 more characters than their standard post length. This is the perfect opportunity to intrigue readers. If you are an artist or musician, people need to know it. A cryptic biography does nothing but confuse a potential follower and could ultimately dissuade one from joining your network.

Lastly, include a link to your home-base, virtual storefront, or product web site. Potential followers may only take one opportunity to visit your web site and see what you represent. It is important to exude a strong professional appearance and demeanor in order to gain followers and the more followers you have, the more trustworthy you and your products appear.

To further garner followers, make sure you display your Twitter user name on your web site, blog, Facebook profile, business cards, newsletters, in forums, and in the signature of your e-mail address. Just notifying existing customers and friends of your Twitter presence can quickly create a loyal fan base.

Twitter Lists

An effective way to organize your followers and to encourage people to follow you is by utilizing the Twitter list feature. Twitter users can organize others into groups, or "lists." When you click to view a list, you'll see a stream of Tweets from all the users included in that group. Each user can have up to 20 lists and each list can have up to 500 members. At the time of the writing of this book, I have 5 lists of visual artists with whom I am networking. This is over 2000 like-minded individuals within my industry and the lists are growing daily. I have several other lists as well that categorize some of the other people I follow or who follow me. You will find that people will often follow your Tweets simply to entice you to include them in your lists.

Another useful aspect of the Twitter list is that you can subscribe to the lists of other users. This allows you to follow an organized group of people in one easy motion. Mentioning a list in a post is as easy as including @<username>/<listname> in a Tweet. This becomes a quick link to a list and can be an excellent way to encourage subscribers and followers.

Hash-tags

A unique posting feature of Twitter is the hash-tag which is simply a number symbol followed by a descriptor. Hash-tags are popular on Twitter because writing space is limited to 140 characters but people can associate their Tweets with an event or product without having to explain the full context. Invented by Chris Messina who was originally with the consulting firm *Citizen Agency*, the first Tweet with a hash-tag read, "how do you feel about using # (pound) for groups. As in #barcamp [msg]?"

Since that initial post, the use of hash-tags has blossomed into an incredible phenomenon. According to Twitter, 11 percent of all Tweets contain at least one hash-tag, pretty amazing considering there are nearly 50 million Tweets posted daily. Hash-tag usage makes Tweets more findable and searchable which is very important in order to gain followers who are interested in your particular business or information. Some of the more commonly used hash-tags and their definitions can be found at the web site http://tagdef.com/.

Often, when I am posting a Tweet regarding a new watercolor painting I have finished, I will post something similar to the following and include various hash-tags as descriptors:

"My latest #watercolor floral #painting uses only 2 pigments, Prussian Blue & Ochre. Not sure if I like the ochre: http://su.pr/33We1j #art"

Notice the usage of #watercolor, #painting, and #art in the post above. By using these hash-tags, users of Twitter who search for watercolor, painting, or art will see my post in the search results. This is a great way to add followers who are interested in the specific information or products that one is representing.

#FollowFriday

One particular hash-tag usage that can be extremely powerful in gaining a follower-base, is #FollowFriday or #FF as it is commonly shortened. When beginning to use the Twitter service it can be a very confusing endeavor deciding who to follow in order to begin developing a network of like-minded individuals. The #FollowFriday hash-tag is a way for fellow Twitter users to help recommend people who they feel are interesting. Whose recommendations would be better to trust than your friends who are already using Twitter?

In mid-January of 2008, Micah Baldwin created the following post which set the #FollowFriday ball rolling:

"I am starting Follow Fridays. Every Friday, suggest a person to follow, and everyone follow him/her. Today its @fancyjeffrey & @wiredone."

Mykl Roventine suggested the #FollowFriday hash-tag and the concept became a perfect example of a crowd-sourced recommendation engine. On the first Follow Friday, there were almost two recommendation Tweets of this nature per second. Current studies indicate that #FollowFriday has now spread into

Thursday and the weekend as well due to the incredible International coverage of the Twitter social-networking service.

There are a couple important news-feed factors to keep in mind when utilizing #FollowFriday. If you are recommending a lot of people, it can become easy to overload the news-feed of your followers. For this reason, I will often use a Tweet scheduler in order to space out the recommendations and define exactly what times I want my Tweets to appear. I use a program called "TweetSched" but there are many online utilities or desktop alternatives. I try to space the #FollowFriday recommendations about three minutes apart since I usually promote about 200 users a week. Three minutes seems to allow ample time to avoid bombarding a follower's news-feed with posts from a single user.

I have found #FollowFriday is most effective when thank you messages are extended to the people that are recommending you to their peers. It is amazing what a little gratitude can accomplish in this world. Knowing you have taken the extra time to thank a fellow Twitter user for their kindness can often prompt them to regularly promote your business or work and can blossom into a mutually productive friendship.

Additionally, when you are planning to follow someone's recommendation, be sure to look at the bio and/or web site of the person being recommended. Often people will use automated services to come up with #FollowFriday lists and this can lead to some unusual suggestions. It is important to maintain a quality group of people you follow and to avoid following those whose content consists solely of meaningless promotions. Quality followers can often mean more than pure numbers. Having said this, I should note that there are many automated responders out there that allow user's to automatically follow new followers, automatically thank new followers, or automatically invite new followers to view a web site, etc... Although these can be convenient, they can frustrate new followers who recognize an automated direct message. The lack of personalization can often lead to losing potential networking opportunities. I would recommend implementing this type of technology with a measure of caution.

Follower Limits

It is important to mention at this juncture that Twitter does impose a following limit. They claim it is the same for all users, regardless of societal stature, so it is important to acknowledge the existence of this rule. Although not officially published, it has been discovered that initially you may only follow a total number of 2001 users until the differential between the number of people you are following and the number of people following you is under 10%. I reached this limit and was forced to "unfollow" several people who weren't following me back in order to allow the followers to catch up with the followed. Once you can maintain this balance, you can continue to follow more people and symbiotically grow your follower-base. It is important to note, however, that these limitations are only imposed upon the number of people you are following. You can have as many followers as there are users who wish to follow you. The following limit is really only in place to minimize problem spamming accounts.

Composing Posts/Tweets

The quality of the information you present to your followers on Twitter or any other social media or blogging service can go to great lengths toward gaining a faithful legion of members. It is important to create pleasant, meaningful, engaging Tweets that are free from inflammatory political or religious rhetoric. Why create polarizing posts that can alienate potential customers simply to make a political or religious statement? In a country like the United States which is, for all intents and purposes, essentially based upon a two-party political system, inflammatory remarks could lose half of a marketer's potential clients. Strong opinions can kill sales and create trust issues. Remember, you are promoting your business and products, not using this venue as a political or religious soapbox. If that is your desire, create a separate non-associated profile for that purpose. More appropriate posts for business promotion would include information about your procedures, techniques, industry data or statistics, or notifications about new product releases, sales, or promotions. This seems like common sense but you wouldn't believe how often people fail to realize that they need to professionally represent themselves in order to be successful. When promoting a business or product, you are not remaining anonymous and while people at the other end of the Internet cable may not be able to physically see you, they can clearly hear your words and their meanings. This can have the same effect as speaking to them directly. It is amazing how many companies have had to fire personnel and have had to expend huge amounts of time and energy simply to undo the damage caused by one ill-conceived social-networking comment written and posted in haste. It is very important to think posts through and to maintain a web-presence based upon professionalism.

Due to the sheer number of people who are using Twitter and the huge numbers of people each person follows, it can be easy for your excellently composed promotional Tweets to become lost in the massive number of posts that move through a user's news feed. Unlike other social-networking services such as Facebook or MySpace, Twitter users may each make from 2 to 20 posts a day. This can create a blur of Tweets running through a user's news feed. Because of this, unlike a lot of social-networking services, this news feed can withstand repeated postings of the same information. I will often post the same notification of a new painting's completion at 7AM, Noon, 8PM, and once the following morning. The key is to make sure the information is seen but to not bombard your followers to the point that they will remove you from their follow lists.

Not only is it important to compose quality, non-offensive and professional Tweets, it is important to recognize the posts of people you are following and to interact with the people in your network. If you expect people to pay attention to your Tweets, you have to return the favor. Remember, you are utilizing this social-networking service to actually "network" with other people who can help promote your product. One great way to do this is to re-Tweet (RT) other members' posts. This is an excellent way to help get their information spread to as many people as possible while helping solidify a great networking relationship with the other member. I usually make sure to thank other Twitter users who do this to my posts and it entices me to re-Tweet their posts as well. It is amazing how far a little kindness and gratitude can take you in the Twitter universe.

If you are interested in seeing a professional ranking of your Twitter efforts, there is a very informative tool located at http://twittergrader.com/ that can help analyze your user name and it's Twitter world effectiveness. Keeping an eye on how your Twitter account's marketing strategy ranks is an effective way to measure your success in the virtual marketing world.

Facebook

What is Facebook?

As of January 2011, Facebook has defined itself as the largest social-networking community of it's kind in the world. Users of the service may create personal profiles, add other users as friends, and exchange messages. According to Facebook's web site, over 50% of the site's active users log in every day and these users spend over 700 billion minutes per month utilizing the service. People on Facebook share more than 30 billion pieces of content every month, including links, news stories, blog posts, and photos. Every month, more than 250 million people engage with Facebook across more than 2.5 million external web sites and the average user clicks the "Like" button 9 times each month. With the addition of third-party applications, users can even integrate existing content from other services into their Facebook pages. RSS feeds, mp3 music players, weather applications, and games are all available to users of Facebook via third-party additions.

Edison research reports that as of June 2011, 51% of Americans over the age of 12 utilize Facebook. However, if you were under the impression that only teenagers utilize the service, think again. The largest segment of Facebook users falls into the 35-54 age range, while the fastest-growing segment is over 55. Regardless of the age of your target demographic, Facebook can be a great way to connect. With a user base of over 500 million people and a 64% market share of the overall social-network service visitation, this is definitely a marketing and networking tool that shouldn't be overlooked and is the perfect way to develop relationships with potential customers.

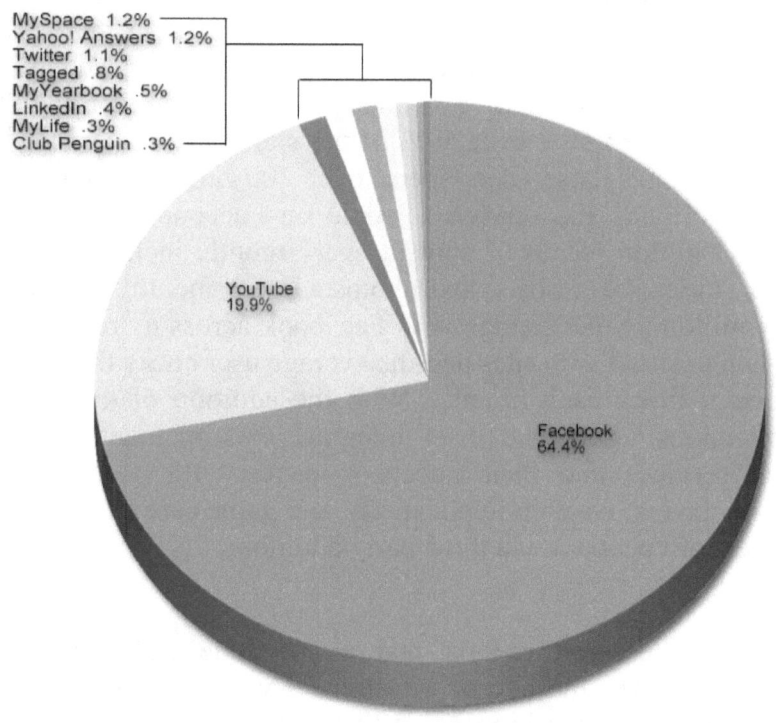

Facebook Marketing Methods

While one might assume that Twitter and Facebook fall into the same category of social-networking service, it needs to be acknowledged that networking techniques that work for one community don't necessarily work for another. Each social-network has its own set of idiosyncrasies that make certain marketing methods more effective than others based upon how information is presented to the subscribers.

In my opinion, Facebook has essentially three main effective ways to market via it's service. These are the Profile, Business Page, and advertisement. You can also market through the use of a Facebook Group but I find this to be relatively ineffective and very time consuming since these are essentially glorified discussion forums. I suspect that it is inevitable that many of the Facebook Group features that exist are going to be integrated into the Business Pages in the future.

The first of these Facebook tools to examine and the initial required component for use of all of these tools is the Facebook Profile. The Profile gives basic information about yourself including age, likes and dislikes, hobbies, education, employment history, and just about anything else you would like to include. It also allows you to supply links to your web sites and is a great way to connect and to share information with family and friends. I love to use mine to share photos with my relatives and occasionally will share information about new paintings and promotions. Generally, however, I prefer to use my profile as a private entity used only to communicate with those close to me such as family, friends, coworkers, and school mates. I only really utilize it as the administrative account for my Facebook Page, however, which is the crux of my Facebook marketing system. It is possible to utilize something Facebook calls a business account to administrate a Business Page but this has very limited functionality so a regular Facebook profile is preferred. It is also important to note that it is a violation of the Facebook *Terms of Service* to operate multiple profile accounts so do not attempt to utilize a business account and personal profile simultaneously in order to have a Business Page or it could result in the termination of your accounts. If that isn't enough of a deterrent, the lack of functionality of a business account should be.

According to Facebook, *"Business accounts are designed for individuals who only want to use the site to administer Pages and their ad campaigns. For this reason, business accounts do not have the same functionality as personal accounts. Business accounts have limited access to information on the site. An individual with a business account can view all the Pages and Facebook Ads that they have created, however they will not be able to view the profiles of users on the site or other content on the site that does not live on the Pages they administer. In addition, business accounts cannot be found in search and cannot send or receive friend requests."*

The Profile

The user name for your profile should be considered carefully when initially creating an account through any social-networking service and Facebook is no exception. It helps if this name is something unique and easily associated with you. Unfortunately, with the sheer number of members using the Facebook service, it is sometimes necessary to be creative in order to find something which hasn't already been used. Be careful in your selection as the only way to undo this is to delete your account which would cause you to lose and have to reestablish connections with everyone with whom you have networked.

The Facebook Profile has many interesting bits of information to supply that can help one find friends with similar interests. It is very helpful to include text describing what it is you do or the focus of the company for which you work, operate, or own. One of the most important aspects of the Facebook information section is the web site link area. Be sure to include links to your central storefront and also any additional web sites that you may have. Don't make your friends on Facebook have to do a general search of the Internet to find your business when they could simply click a link you have supplied. I often have people who stop by and "Like" my Business Page and I simply can't find their Business Pages or web sites because they have not thought to leave links to them on their Facebook profile.

While many people have successfully used the Facebook profile to promote their businesses, the main deterrents to using it as your only social-networking marketing tool, are the limitations that have been intentionally engineered into it. The Facebook profile limits the number of friends you can have to 5000. Additionally, there has to be a mutual relationship between you and your friends in order for information to be shared. In other words, you have to approve friendships with people before they can see your products and business information. With a huge number of Facebook "lurkers," or non-interacting members, requiring a friendship to view your product essentially excludes a large percentage of possible clients.

An additional, and probably the most important, downside to marketing through a Facebook profile, is that profiles are excluded from being publicly searched by Google which can severely limit the potential number of people who can view your profile and therefore, the products you are selling. Remember that you are trying to get your products, services, storefront, or artwork in front of as many people as possible in order to statistically increase the potential of sales.

Another even stronger reason to avoid using a Facebook profile to promote or market products or services is that it is actually a breach of the Facebook *Terms of Service* and it is quite possible an account could be suspended if Facebook deemed it necessary. According to Facebook,

"All personal site features, such as friending and messaging, are for personal use only and may not be used for professional promotion. If you add a user as a friend, for example, this person will be invited to be a friend of your profile and not your Page. Using personal site features for professional promotion, or creating unauthorized Pages, may result in your account being warned or disabled."

Facebook specifically created another tool for businesses to utilize and there are some very good reasons to use it instead of your profile as your main selling vehicle. This tool is known as the Facebook Business Page and was designed specifically for businesses, artists, and musicians to connect with their fans without requiring a mutual relationship approval. Users can simply "Like" the Business Page in order to receive updates in their news feed.

The Business Page

Facebook created a specific type of presence for businesses, musicians, and artists to utilize for networking and interacting with customers and fans because these entities often have thousands of fans with which they need to interact. Can you imagine a large corporation with potentially millions of fans of a product having to approve every relationship in order to market promotions, coupons, or advancements? Although many of us may never reach this level of fame, Facebook Business Pages have been designed to allow the incorporation of many amazing tools to help one sell their products and to network with other users in the same manner as many large corporations.

The Facebook Business Page allows for multiple people with profiles to be administrators of the same account which can be useful if you have multiple aspects of a business which need to be updated by several people. You may have one administrator posting weekly coupons and another posting interesting Research and Development (R&D) information while still another is handling polls, lotteries, and product trivia. The possibilities are virtually limitless.

The Facebook Business Page has many advantages over the Profile for marketing and one of the most important is the lack of a 5000 follower limit. Additionally, a Page's administrator needs not approve friendships before people are allowed to view a Page's information. Users can easily "Like" a Page by clicking a button which instantly allows updates to be included in their news feed. Facebook has designed this to be as simple as possible. Additionally, because Business Pages are public, they can be crawled by search engines such as Google or Bing which can cause a greater web presence for you or your product. This can ultimately result in more traffic to your Facebook Page and more traffic to the central node of your marketing network. These pages show near the top of major search engine results which is an even stronger endorsement for why you need to have a Business Page to market your products and company.

The downside to the Facebook Business Page, however, is that it often requires a bit more effort to build a fan base as one needs to establish a clear foothold within the Facebook community. Getting it to work well takes time, dedication, and planning. One should not expect to create a Business Page and then instantaneously have a huge following. If you create great content, make it easy to share, and make people aware of it's presence, over time your network will grow. Luckily, there are some important and productive things one can do in order to entice more fans over a shorter amount of time.

Business Page Marketing

Facebook Business Pages have been designed to be virtually a stand-alone entity. Facebook does not really want to encourage people to navigate away from their service because they are continually serving demographically targeted advertisements to viewers of the pages. Because of this, however, Facebook has created some remarkable tools for one to utilize in order to market products that can be integrated into each Business Page. Although the Page can generate some traffic to your central storefront, don't expect a Facebook Business Page to be your main traffic generator. It is effective in directing some traffic to the central node of your Internet-based marketing approach, but the bulk of Facebook's usefulness is internal to it's community. Because it is such a great vehicle for selling products and because it has such a large community of users, it is important to develop a base of followers to which one can market.

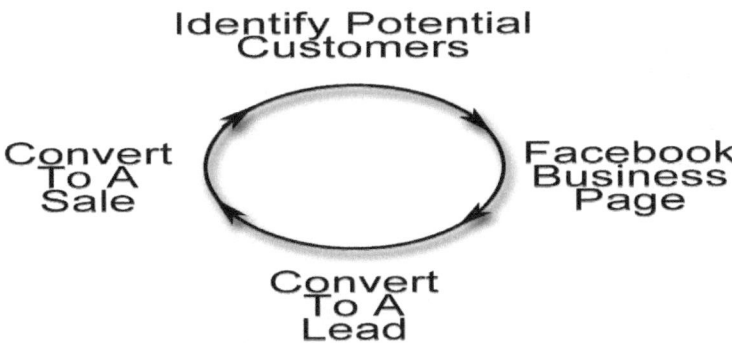

As I stated earlier, a Facebook Business Page, although clearly the best approach for marketing through this particular social-networking service, can often be a difficult entity to which to attract followers. There are a few key things you can do to ease this process which can help establish an initial foothold in the community.

Begin by making full use of the information section available for the Business Page. This is where one should make it clear what the company does, what the product is, and any other interesting details that set you apart from the competition. Let people know who you are and be sure to include links to your other social-network presences as well as your main storefront. Often, users of one social-networking service will be using others and will want to connect with you through their other Internet presences. This will allow you to access a follower's network across multiple venues and can greatly increase your product's visibility.

Include a link to your Facebook Business Page from your profile. Don't make users hunt to find your business. Additionally, Facebook will automatically make a link to your Facebook Business Page from your profile if you indicate your current occupation is your Business Page. For example, I have set the occupation on my Facebook profile as Ken Powers so at the top of my Profile, Ken Powers is listed as where I work and this is automatically a link to my artist Business Page which is located at http://www.facebook.com/powersfineart.

Custom Tabs & Landing Pages

One of the interesting features of the Facebook Business Page that once existed for profiles but was removed in 2011, is the ability to add custom tabs. Facebook removed these from profiles in order to encourage usage of the Business Pages. The ability to have custom tabs has opened the door to allow anything from third-party selling tools to custom-coded applications and embedded HTML pages utilizing inline frames. Essentially, if you are not using a third-party application tab, you can use HTML inline frames to display an externally hosted HTML page. Although the actual creation of these pages is beyond the scope of this text, there are many tutorials available online that can walk one through the process. Additionally, there are even services that can create and host the embedded external pages.

One of the most important uses for the custom tab is the creation of a landing page. This is essentially the first page people see if they are not currently "Liking" your Business Page and is set in the Page's preferences. It is designed to be an advertisement that entices Facebook users to "Like" your Page. While the standard landing page is set to your Facebook wall, statistical analysis has shown that a custom landing page can easily double the number of first-time viewers who choose to "Like" your Business Page. There is no shame in self-promotion for this page since it is an advertisement for your business and products. Make it clear what information is being presented to "Fans" of this particular Business Page and don't feel uncomfortable about promoting about yourself. While it may seem egotistical to promote yourself in this manner within your Facebook profile, it is just plain good business to sell yourself on the landing tab of your Business Page. The idea is to create interest in what you have to offer people in their news feed and having a custom landing page gives you an important initial opportunity to present that information to first-time viewers. On my fine art Business Page at http://www.facebook.com/powersfineart, my landing tab has a very simple embedded HTML page that randomly picks three pieces of artwork from my portfolio, displays my logo, provides links to my other web presences, and notifies users that clicking "Like" will get updates from me on their Facebook wall in the form of artwork, marketing tips, and networking aids. This custom tab has proven itself to be highly effective in enticing fans to "Like" my Business Page and I highly recommend the use of this tool.

Your Page's Profile Picture

Choosing a professional image to represent your new Business Page can be a difficult decision. Not only does it need to be professional, but it also needs to clearly represent you, your company, and your product. One might think it is as simple as uploading a picture of yourself and moving on. However, Facebook actually permits you to accomplish considerably more customization.

At the time of this writing, Facebook allows the Business Page profile image to be 540 pixels high by 180 pixels wide. This means that you can get far more creative than simply uploading a head shot or product photo. By using a graphics manipulation program such as Photoshop, you can use this added screen real estate to add graphical text, company logos, web site addresses, and anything else you can imagine in a 540 pixel by 180 pixel portrait oriented image.

This is a great place to get creative and incorporate your company's brand, etc... On my Page, I chose to put my logo, three framed pieces of artwork, and one large image that changes occasionally based upon my mood or current promotion. This section of the graphic is the one that gets seen as my avatar when I create posts or comments on Facebook. I also have a small section of text on the image that lets people know that I am a watercolor artist who creates commission work and sells original paintings and prints. Even though it is not clickable, I have also included the URL of my main website to help tie my Facebook Page together with my centralized marketing strategy.

Often, I recommend including a head shot in this image as it helps to have a photo to aid in connecting with potential fans and friends. People often respond in a more positive manner to a friendly face. Additionally, mentioning your company's core offering can be a great way to help immediately let people know what you have to offer them. As I stated above, I mentioned what it is that I do and what I can offer clients when I constructed my Page's image. Bear in mind that most of the time once people have "Liked" your page, they won't regularly come back and will be mainly viewing your posts in their news feed. For this reason, having a great profile picture and creating an excellent first impression is very important.

It is a smart idea to investigate what people who are in a similar industry are putting in their profile picture in order to see what possibilities exist. Try to incorporate some original concepts and see if modifications you make create spikes in "Likes" or "Unlikes" of your Business Page by viewing the available Analytics that Facebook has to offer.

Once you have chosen the image to represent you, your company, and products or services, it is time to get busy creating useful content for your Facebook fans to read and to engage in conversation.

Provide Great Content

Before you begin developing a following with any social-networking service, you need to realize that people won't be coming back to visit your Page or read your posts unless you have something to offer them. Believe it or not, content is the key to success and great content keeps users returning to see what you are going to unveil next. Constant meaningless posts will encourage fans to leave you quickly. In fact, according to a study by *ExactTarget*, 55% of Facebook users admit to "UnLiking" or "Hiding" Business Pages from their feeds for one of the following three reasons related to over-posting:

1. Their news feed became cluttered with "Thank-You" notes and "Welcome" messages by the Business Page to new Fans.

2. A Business Page had been sending a large series of posts over a very short amount of time.

3. A Business Page posted too many times during the course of a single day.

Obviously this study makes it clear that one needs to consider very carefully how often and when to post Facebook updates. With followers of a page living in an age where time is a valuable commodity, people desire to quickly access their account, briefly peruse the updates of their friends, and move on to the rest of the business of the day. For this reason, it is important to consider very carefully the quality of the information that you are presenting to those who are Fans of your Business Page.

It is critical for one to realize that everything posted on a Business Page will show up in the news feeds of everyone who "Likes" the Page. For this reason, many of the rules for composing useful Tweets for Twitter apply to the Facebook realm as well. Maintaining a courteous and professional relationship with those who follow your Page will cause your network to continue to grow and flourish. After all, the entire reason you are utilizing social-networking to market your products is to reach as many people as possible and to receive real-time feed-back. For this reason, one's posts to any social-network need to be designed to attract followers, not to drive them away.

I have mentioned it once in this text and I believe it bears repeating. Compose meaningful, useful, engaging posts that are free from political and religious rhetoric. Several surveys have been conducted which asked people what types of Facebook posts aggravated them the most and caused them to stop following a brand. As you might imagine, the results were not a surprise.

The top three reasons people revealed for "unliking" a page or "unfriending" a Facebook user were determined to be the following:

1. Posting too frequently.

2. Sharing unsolicited political or religious views.

3. Inappropriate posts that are crude or racist.

Remember, you are promoting a business and it is necessary to remain courteous and professional. Effective posts should include coupon codes, current promotions, links to interesting industry-related articles, new product announcements, and possibly even cross-promotional links to other businesses. Create tutorials to instruct people in the use of different software packages, tips and tricks for using Facebook or other services, or even instructions for setting up an online storefront through one of the many popular Internet services. Produce videos depicting your creative processes, share some of your favorite books, and even write product or equipment reviews. Realize that you are trying to create engaging content that will elicit repeat visitation by your fans.

Encouraging interaction with your followers by asking questions and creating dialog can be key to developing follower loyalty. It can also aid in enticing followers to share links to your page and products which can cause an increase in followership. If your content is so great that it causes people to share it with their friends, you are bound to have them repeatedly coming back for more.

Avoid spamming your followers. Include more in your posts than continual product promotion. If a person is bombarded by continual promotional information with no useful content, they are going to quickly "unlike" your Business Page. Individuals are inundated with continual spam in their e-mail accounts already. Don't subject them to more in their Facebook news feed.

Include images as often as possible when you are composing posts. When you post links on Facebook, you are usually presented with a thumbnail option for the resulting site. When people are following as many as 500 pages, it is easy for your post to get lost in the convoluted blur of their news feed. Having an image makes the post stand out and will definitely encourage more interaction from fans. When they say a picture is worth a thousand words, they mean it. At the very least, having a picture will draw attention to your content.

If you are unsure if your updates are creating the proper results, then realize that Facebook offers some of the most amazing tools in the social-networking world to analyze your successes and failures. Look at these analytical tools and search for trends. If you see a large jump or drop in followers or interactions during a specific time-period, look at the posts you have made and adjust accordingly. If something you have posted causes a sudden loss of fans, then you need to avoid that type of post in the future. Give your fans and followers what they want. We are not utilizing this service to offend, we are using it to network with like-minded individuals who enjoy what we have to offer them. It is this spirit of communication and connection that will cause your network to grow instead of dwindling or remaining stagnant.

Use Facebook as Page

Approximately March of 2011, Facebook introduced a new feature that allows a Business Page's administrator to utilize Facebook as their Business Page and not their Profile. What is great about this is that one can now make comments on other Pages, "Like" other Pages, and interact with other Pages as one's business. When another Page's administrator or fan looks at who "Liked" their latest post and they see your business, artist, or musician Page name, this is a link back to your Business Page. Viewers of these other Page's will see your Page's interaction and may be enticed to click the link to see who you are. This is a very effective way to network with other businesses as your brand and it can create fantastic cross-promotional opportunities.

Although "Liking" another Page's post may indicate that you are interested in their content and what they have to say, there is not a substitute for an actual comment, dialog, and interaction with the Page's administrator and fans in order to draw followers to your Business Page.

Be wary of posting links to your business' Page directly on another Business Page's wall. Although many Page's, like mine, encourage it, some administrators frown upon it. There are much better approaches and this type of brazen attempt to hijack followers can often be considered poor protocol. Often posts of this type will get completely deleted by the administrator of the Page and, quite frankly, they could be construed as unprofessional and a form of spam. There are much better approaches to enticing fans from another Business Page to follow your business which don't create tension and are actually mutually beneficial. Cross-promotional techniques are much more effective and not only help you expand your customer network but also your inter-industry network which can often be even more important in the long-term. I have said it before and I will say it again, never forget the importance of maintaining a professional persona when it comes to presenting yourself, products, and business to potential Internet-based clients and comrades.

Use of the "@" Symbol

In 2009, Facebook added a feature that allows you to mention a fellow Facebook user or Page in a status update or post. In 2011, they further expanded the usability of this feature to include mentions in comments on posts as well. This is Facebook's most Twitter-like feature to date and has amazing possibilities.

The way this works is simple. When you are writing a post and wish to mention another user or Business Page for a cross-promotional purpose, you simple type the "@" symbol and a drop-down menu will appear that allows you to pick a Page, user, group, or event from the list. The feature includes auto-suggest, so as you type after the "@" symbol, Facebook lets you select users from a drop-down menu. Meanwhile, after you've tagged someone in an update, they get a notification, as well as a post on their wall. This is a fantastic way to discretely gain followers through cross-promotional techniques as the mention becomes an active link to the Page or user.

I have several industry acquaintances with whom I have connected who have decided to pick a particular day of the week to cross-promote other artists whose work we admire. This has not only made our own fans aware of the work of others, but has also gained us followers who are simply interested not only in our work, but also the work of people we find interesting. This is the very foundation of social-networking and use of the "@" symbol for mentions only furthers the size of the network. The great thing about this is that you aren't just limited to using it as your profile, but you can also use it as your Business Page. This means that mentions that appear on other Business Pages' or users' walls also contain your business avatar and Facebook Business Page link.

As you can see, this is a much better technique to use to gain additional followers than to directly post a "come check me out" link on someone's wall. The Facebook mention helps out everyone who is involved and you often find that people are flattered and appreciate that you would endeavor to cross-promote their work or products and they return the favor. I make sure to take the time to thank and cross-promote the people and businesses that make this effort on my behalf and it is a fantastic feeling to lend a helping hand to another member of one's social-network.

Product Specific Content

Facebook offers so many great ways to present information about one's products or services and it is important to take advantage of them in order to present useful content to followers. You can use the video tab to advance interesting presentations about your products, business, artwork, or music and you can create interesting dialog by utilizing the discussion tab. Additionally, there are many third-party applications available to present your products to your fans. A couple great examples are *Reverbnation,* for musicians, which allows music to be played and songs to be sold as well as the *Fine Art America* Shop tab which allows artwork displayed in the Print on Demand service, *Fine Art America*, to be displayed and prints to be sold. These are just two examples but there are literally thousands of others from which to pick depending upon what you wish to accomplish.

One of the most important built-in Facebook tabs for product promotion, however, is the Photo tab. This is a great area to create albums of images specific to photographs of various aspects of your products and business. I use mine to create albums of artwork which pertain to each series I am painting. I also like to include credit line information for each piece that stays with the artwork when it is viewed. This includes a Copyright notice, the size of the work, and the materials used.

Since Facebook doesn't provide titles for the images, adding this information is critical for potential sales.

Facebook Ads

Facebook provides some incredible tools for serving demographically targeted advertisements to its constituents. Being able to utilize some pretty powerful targeting parameters, you can create ads aimed at specific geographic areas, age groups, and even college major. The company also lets users "Like" ads or close ads they don't like. This means that Facebook is continually delivering increasingly better-targeted ads to their users. The advertisements are placed to the right of a user's news feed and are very unobtrusive. You will find an example of what the ads look like below. If you choose to utilize this tool, you can choose how long you want the ad to run, the text presented, and even how you wish to pay for it.

Example Facebook Advertisement

Ken Powers

Visit and "Like" the Page of Tacoma, WA watercolor artist Ken Powers for great artwork and helpful marketing tips to aid your business!

👍 Like • Ken Powers likes this.

One can choose to pay per 1000 impressions or per actual ad click. You essentially bid how much you would like to pay for the ad and if you win the automated auction for the specific time, your ad will be shown. The downside is that this can get fairly expensive to continually utilize. Although Facebook ads may be a great way to jump-start the growth of a Page, organic growth is more likely to create a more engaged fan base. Ads are a feature that may work better for some product types than others. However, it may be the perfect thing to notify local people of an upcoming event you are hosting or in which you are participating. Serving ads for notification of a new product release or an amazingly discounted promotion may be just the thing to push your business' social-network presence over the top.

Google+

Why Use Google+?

Although Google+ is in it's Beta testing phase at the time of this writing, it is a networking service that cannot be ignored. Within it's first 16 days of usage, it had already gained a user base of over 10 million people. It's subscriber base is exponentially growing faster than any social-network to date and it's growth is currently being managed by a controlled number of current user invitations. With Google's strong backing, once the service is released for public usage, it is bound to become one of the most popular social-networks available. For this reason, Google+ will be an excellent foundation upon which to stage product marketing campaigns.

The Google+ social-network has a very comfortable user interface and much of it's functionality combines the best parts of the networks in whose tracks it follows. It has a news feed called a Stream which is very similar to both Twitter and Facebook. It incorporates Google's +1 button which acts in a similar fashion to Facebook's "Like" feature but also moves a post back to the top of a user's Stream which creates a functionality very similar to Twitter's Re-Tweet. Cleverly timing responses to comments and adding +1's to user's feedback can be a an effective way to increase a product or post's visibility. In theory, the best content will have increased visibility simply from social-determination. The posts seem to behave like a Twitter feed but have an appearance much like a

Facebook post. It is essentially the best of both worlds. Because of the large number of posts that pass through a user's Stream, Google+ feeds can withstand more frequent sharing of the same information much in the same fashion as Twitter.

Due to what is essentially a crowd-sourced post ranking system, it is necessary to make sure each and every post and promotion presented through this service counts or they could easily get lost in the Stream. Once again, quality posts that contain original engaging content are the key to success.

The Google+ Profile

As with all social-networks, it is very important to make sure the user profile is filled out in it's entirety. There is nothing more frustrating than gaining a new follower and not being able to determine their occupation or interests. Since Google+'s main follower organizational tool is known as a circle, don't make it hard for followers to determine in which of their circles to place you or your business.

Another reason to fill out your profile page properly is that your profile actually shows up in Google's search engine results. The title that is displayed comes from your Google+ profile name and the description comes from the introduction field. With such a high degree of visibility, it is important to not neglect such a basic element of this social-network.

Another useful feature on the profile page is the ability to individually adjust the visibility of each section. Every element can be set so it can be visible to everyone on the web, your circle of friends, extended circles of friends, or even more specific custom permissions. This unique approach to security and permissions puts nearly every detail in control of the account owner.

Circles and Posts

A unique feature of Google+ is that it has a very interesting way to categorize one's followers. Users create circles in which people with similar criteria can be grouped. Family members can be placed in one circle, potential product purchasers can be placed in another, and friends can be placed in yet another. One can create many circles and each can have a particular focus.

The extremely effective aspect of this concept, and one of Google+'s main selling points, is that posts can be specifically directed toward one or more of these categorized groups of people. Photos of candid moments can be directed only toward friends or specific individuals while important business promotions can be directed only toward a circle of potential purchasers. It is even possible to direct a post to a single viewer which could make the Google+ posts a substitute for many other direct messaging formats. The posts can include links or media and can be edited at any time.

Based around controlled data visibility, this functionality creates a very flexible messaging system while keeping private information in front of a very specific group of people. The circle concept has great marketing potential in that product promotions or feedback could be directed toward a very specific group of people instead of everyone on the World Wide Web.

Discount codes could be presented to a circle of repeat clients while promotional coupons could be directed toward the general public. Pre-release versions of products, music, or artwork could be aimed at influential circles without alerting the general public. The possibilities that exist for this type of limited sharing are endless.

Presentation of Media

Google+ has some really well-designed media presentation tools available. Whether it involves a nice thumbnail to accompany a link, a product photograph, or an instructional video, Google+ can accommodate.

Videos and photographs can be placed in albums and can be shared to individual users or multiple circles. Additionally, the ability to re-share the information or comment upon its content can be enabled or disabled. Each piece of media can be accompanied by a caption to describe the photo. Additionally, viewers may comment and leave feedback if desired. This is a very effective way to receive real-time information about new products or promotions. As viewers comment or choose to give the image a +1, the image will move to the top of a user's viewable Stream. In this way, the photograph or video can continue to remain visible instead of being lost in an endless barrage of information. It is important to note, however, that Google+'s algorithms tend to favor newer content when information is presented to user's in their Stream. Theoretically, better content with more feedback and sharing will bubble to the top of the feed.

YouTube

What is YouTube?

YouTube was created by three former PayPal employees in 2005 and is a service that allows users to upload, view, and search for video clips. The company was purchased in 2006 by Google, Inc. and as of 2010 accounts for 28% of all Internet searches. Alexa, which is a site that provides web site metrics and analytic data, actually ranks YouTube as the third most visited site in the world, trailing only behind Google and Facebook.

Because of the extreme popularity of this service, it can be a great vehicle for generating and directing traffic to your central storefront. By posting product demonstrations, musical performance clips, time-lapse videos, or demonstrations one can easily promote one's business through this network. I should note that simply uploading a commercial is something that YouTube doesn't really allow and is likely to be removed. Because of this, one has to be more creative in their approach.

I am not going to focus too much on the "how-to's" of using this service, but with the sheer number of videos that exist on YouTube, it is easy to get lost in the mix. Like any other social-networking community, it is important to participate. Become friends with other members and subscribe to their content. Believe it or not, YouTube is another social-network where people can comment on videos and give them a "Thumbs-Up" or "Thumbs-Down." Many of the techniques that apply to Twitter and Facebook apply to YouTube as well. As you have learned by now, participation and cross-promotion are the keys to social-network success. Since YouTube is a social-network community, it is necessary to spend time commenting on the videos of other members and forging relationships. Make sure your videos contain links to your web site, central-node, or storefront as this is how you are going to direct traffic back to a page where you can actually sell your products or promote your business.

When you create your YouTube account, there is an information section to complete. Like all the social-networking sites of which we have spoken previously, it is necessary to fill in as much of this data as possible while keeping it very professional. Choose an appropriate profile picture, be sure to provide a link to your central storefront in the web site URL section, and be clear and concise in describing yourself and your business in the "About Me" area.

Probably the most important thing to know about posting videos on YouTube is to make sure you choose appropriate tags which identify the video content. Since I am promoting artwork and my videos are often time-lapse demonstrations of the creation of specific works, my video tags are usually something similar to: art, fine-art, watercolor, floral, painting, etc... These tags are what allow the search engines to find your videos and if neglected, will leave your videos viewer-less.

Another important thing to consider is the short attention span of the modern Internet user. For this reason, I have found that if videos are kept fairly short, they are more likely to be viewed in their entirety. My ten minute videos are very rarely watched to completion while my films that are under two minutes are sometimes watched multiple times by the same viewer. The idea is to get the information to the recipient through the quickest means possible and video is a fantastic way to accomplish that goal.

LinkedIn

Why Utilize LinkedIn?

LinkedIn is generally known as the world's largest business social-network. It is designed to allow business and industry professionals to connect with each other and to allow professionals in any given industry to manage their professional identities and to build an industry specific network. Additionally, the service allows one to continually remain informed. Incredibly, LinkedIn has been adopted globally with nearly 2 billion people searches in 2010 and over 90 million users in January 2011.

It is easy to think of LinkedIn as strictly a site you visit when you need to find a new occupation and LinkedIn has been continually fighting that perception. However, the service has much more to offer and can aid in creating some very valuable business connections and marketing opportunities. Luckily, there are some important things one can do in order to increase their LinkedIn profile visibility.

It is very important to keep your LinkedIn profile current in order to highlight your experience and expertise. It can serve as a great way to share your history with other LinkedIn members and anyone online. Interestingly, LinkedIn profiles often manifest themselves very highly in Internet search results.

Be certain to participate in the available LinkedIn groups. They are a fantastic way to identify and network with other users who have similar interests. Additionally, the LinkedIn groups allow you to view contact information of other users. By participating, one can easily begin establishing a reputation as being an expert in any given field. Discussions can be viewed by anyone on the web and even show up in Internet search engine results.

Another aspect of LinkedIn that shouldn't be overlooked, is the ability to have a recommendation by a business or acquaintance linked to your profile. Word of mouth reputation holds an enormous amount of credibility when viewed by potential clients. By collecting a series of success stories, one can create a testimonial page that can lead to very beneficial future opportunities.

LinkedIn offers an amazing amount of features without having to resort to utilizing their premium membership. It is easy to set up, easy to maintain, and doesn't require a large investment in time. With such a rich feature set, LinkedIn should not be overlooked as an essential part of your online networking and marketing strategy.

StumbleUpon

What is StumbleUpon?

I have saved one of my favorite traffic generating social-networking community sites for last. Out of all the social-communities to which I belong, StumbleUpon, or SU as it is known, generates by far the largest amount of traffic to my central storefront. With a user base of over 15 million at the time of this writing, one has to wonder what will happen as the site continues to grow in membership. It is quite unique in its functionality compared to the other social-networks with which I have experimented but the results have been incredible. I would feel very confident in proclaiming StumbleUpon to be the Internet's premier social-bookmarking service and would highly recommend it's usage for product promotion.

StumbleUpon is more technically being described as a discovery or recommendation engine, as opposed to a search engine, that finds and delivers content to its users based upon their specifically specified tastes and interests using peer-sourcing and social-networking principles. StumbleUpon uses a process known as collaborative filtering to combine user choices with service-learned user browsing preferences. What is interesting about this is that by choosing people to follow in the community, this influences the genres of web site that are shown when you browse via StumbleUpon. You are viewing pages that have been explicitly recommended by your friends in the community. Because of this, one can recommend their own pages to the community as well. Every time I have finished posting a new painting, I add it to the StumbleUpon community and appropriately tag it so it will be presented to StumbleUpon members who are interested in artistic content.

As with any social-network, the timing of posts, shares, or recommendations is very important. According to StumbleUpon research from April 2011:

1. *Stumbling increases very quickly in the morning commute hours, and mobile plays a big part in that – during this time, mobile stumbling is 70% higher than the daily mobile stumbling average.*
2. *There is an inverse relationship between what gets stumbled during work hours and what gets stumbled in the evening. Some of the most popular topics during work hours are Cars, Technology, and Health. Some of the most popular topics stumbled at night are Relationships and Philosophy.*
3. *Users stumble at work only 20% less than off the clock. But users still stumble once every 3 minutes on average while at work.*

Increasing StumbleUpon Traffic

Based upon the premise that *"people don't purchase items which they don't know exist,"* increasing traffic to your site is of the highest importance and that is exactly what StumbleUpon can accomplish. Adding your site or pages to the StumbleUpon system and encouraging members of the community to give them a "Thumbs-Up" will increase their presence in the StumbleUpon randomization engine. The better the pages are ranked, the more frequently they will appear.

Obviously, just adding your page to the StumbleUpon community isn't going to make it an instantaneous success but it is the first step one needs to take in order to reach that goal. StumbleUpon expects you to maintain an active presence in their community and there are a few things you can do to achieve that. You can be active by discovering web sites, reviewing them, and by giving each site a "Thumbs-Up" or "Thumbs-Down." StumbleUpon's randomization engine suggests your discoveries to its users based upon the activity of your account so being an active member will definitely aid in increasing the presence of your own pages in the community.

After submitting a page to StumbleUpon, the service tests the popularity of your submission by driving a few users to your content. If your submitted page receives favorable response from these users, it will be suggested to many more. Requesting a "Thumbs-Up" from your friends in the community within the first days of submission can really aid in increasing the content's exposure.

Obviously, as with any social-networking site, it is necessary to develop a network of followers and friends. By following members of the StumbleUpon community and allowing information to be shared with them, you are taking a great step toward further promoting your products and pages. Creating a base of friends within the community with whom one can share their page submissions increases the probability that new content will receive viewer approval and therefore increased StumbleUpon exposure.

For example, I once posted a completed painting on a Sunday morning and immediately added it to the StumbleUpon system. I then posted a link about it on Twitter and then Facebook. Within two days the image had been viewed 1985 times. Out of those 1985 times, Google Analytics showed that the page had been navigated to from StumbleUpon 987 times, from Twitter 376 times, and from Facebook 76 times. The remaining 546 visitors originated from within Fine Art America where the image was posted. As you can see, StumbleUpon generated an incredible amount of traffic compared to the other social-networking sites. Interestingly, the original sold within a day of posting and was purchased by a StumbleUpon user. Although this doesn't happen with every painting I post, StumbleUpon is still the highest traffic generator of all the networking sites which I utilize.

StumbleUpon, like many other social-networking sites, also allows you to include a badge or link on your web site, blog, or other Internet presence which can help notify viewers of your StumbleUpon profile.

Su.pr Link Shortener

Due to the increasing number of social-networking sites that limit the number of characters composing a post, there has been the creation of multiple services that will shorten the URL of a link and use redirection to send traffic to the link's destination. Several of the more popular services that exist are bit.ly, Tiny URL and goog.gl. Many of these offer analytic capabilities but my favorite is Su.pr which is StumbleUpon's link shortener and can be found at http://su.pr/.

One of the advantages of using the Su.pr link shortener is that you can post a link directly to Twitter, your Facebook Profile, and your Facebook Page from a single page on the service. Additionally, you can immediately add the page to StumbleUpon, categorize the page, and add a review. Due to it's convenience and integration into StumbleUpon, you can cover a lot of ground in one fell swoop. Additionally, StumbleUpon makes it no secret that utilizing this link shortening service will increase the presence of your pages within it's randomization engine.

Su.pr also offers some pretty amazing analytics capabilities to it's users. Based upon the performance of your links, you can see what times are best to post URL's to social-networking services, how many link clickers are Stumblers, and how many are from other sources. If you are using the sharing feature of StumbleUpon to share pages you like with other users of the service, Su.pr's analytics will also show you which Stumblers liked the page you shared.

Account Security

Help, I've Been Hacked!

This is something that I seldom see addressed when speaking of social-networking but is of major concern. Any time you have an account through one of these services, there is always the possibility that an unauthorized user can gain access. It is best to avoid this possibility, however, by making sure you use secure passwords and changing them frequently. Believe it or not, people like to use simple words they can remember for their account password and often will use the same password for all accounts they use. If these words can be found in a dictionary, there are many automated tools that exist for easily attempting to gain access to your account by repeatedly choosing passwords from a dictionary list. You can drastically decrease the possibility of this type of attack being successful by simply choosing more complicated passwords. Use longer passwords and include numbers and special characters. If you insist on using a word or combination of words from the dictionary, consider replacing the i's with 1's and the o's with 0's and, at the very least, use a special character such as a -,?,or $ symbol to make things more complicated to guess or hack.

In the remote circumstance where your account has been compromised on one of the social-networking services, the most important thing you need to do is immediately change your password. If the hacker has been smart enough to change your password for you, most services have a link that will send your password to your email address. Often this will simply say something similar to "Forgot your password?" Immediately click the link, have the password sent to your email account, use the password to access your social-networking service account, and immediately change your password to something more secure. If your email address has been compromised as well, you will then need to navigate to the social-network site's security page where you will need to submit a report. Most of the time, however, your email address will not have been modified and this technique will be successful.

Once you have regained control of the account, make sure to create several posts that indicate to your followers or fans what has recently happened and that you now have the situation rectified. It is important to instill confidence in your followers that this incident in no way has compromised their accounts as well. It may take some time to perform this damage control but it is well worth it. It is very possible that you will have lost some followers due to the incident but at least make an attempt to save the ones you have.

If you are unfortunate enough to have your account compromised, use the experience as an important lesson and make every effort in the future to use secure passwords which are frequently changed.

Conclusion

Final Remarks and Insights

Very frequently I hear people complain about how the service where they have chosen to display their products weights their internal search results so only certain items appear within the first pages. Often sites will do this in order to display items or work which they feel best represent the image they wish to portray to their purchasing clientele. Unfortunately, if your work doesn't fall into the site's narrow definition of what it wants to use to represent itself, your sales are going to be seriously affected. Remember, *"People don't purchase products they don't know exist."*

This is a perfect example of how utilizing social-networking can completely change the playing field. By directing your own traffic to your work and products, you are removing that particular web site's local site search engine from the equation. Further, the traffic you send is generally going to be interested in your products and your products alone and not a general sampling of what the particular web site has to offer. This alone should be a convincing endorsement for utilizing a social-network marketing strategy.

Blindly entering into the social-networking world, however, can be ineffective if one proceeds without a plan. Hopefully the previous chapters of this text have presented a clear Internet marketing philosophy based around a central storefront marketing strategy and has introduced you to the effectiveness of the incorporation of social-media. Remember, however, creating a useful system of connected networks requires an investment of time and dedication for which there is no substitute. The tips and methods presented in the previous sections of this book should aid you on your journey to quickly developing a network but maintaining it and nurturing it are your responsibility.

Index

Alphabetical Index

Administrator..79, 95, 96
Analytics...87, 128, 132
Anchor text..33, 34
Apple..50
Bing..29, 38, 80, 116
Blog...9, 54, 65, 71, 129
Brand..44, 49, 50, 53, 85, 90, 95
Business Page...73, 74, 75, 77, 79, 80, 81, 82, 83, 84, 85, 87, 89, 90, 92, 95, 96, 97, 98
Circle...107, 109, 110, 111
CRM..49
Deep linking..33
Ebay..22
Etsy..22
Facebook....16, 17, 18, 38, 41, 43, 46, 49, 54, 66, 69, 71, 73, 74, 75, 76, 77, 79, 80, 81, 82, 83, 84, 85, 86, 87, 89, 90, 91, 92, 95, 97, 98, 99, 100, 101, 102, 105, 106, 115, 116, 128, 131
Fan Page..46
Fine Art America..99, 128
FollowFriday..59, 60
Google 29, 30, 37, 38, 76, 80, 103, 105, 106, 107, 109, 111, 115, 128
Google+...103, 105, 106, 107, 109, 111
Hacked...135
Hacker..135
Hash-tag...57, 58, 59
HTML...22, 28, 29, 83, 84
Inbound links..33

Interlink..33, 34
Interlinking...33
Internet...9, 15, 17, 18, 21, 22, 27, 30, 38, 43, 65, 75, 81, 82, 91, 96, 115, 117, 121, 122, 125, 129, 139
Link exchange...31, 33
Link shortener...131
LinkedIn...16, 119, 121, 122
Lists...55, 56, 60, 66
Lurkers..49, 76
Media....16, 17, 37, 41, 42, 43, 44, 45, 46, 53, 65, 109, 111, 128, 131, 140
Mp3..71
MySpace..16, 17, 66
Outbound links...33
Password...135, 136
PayPal..115
PDF...9
Photograph..99, 111
Photos...22, 49, 71, 74, 85, 109
Photoshop..85
Profile...16, 17, 37, 38, 46, 54, 65, 71, 73, 74, 75, 76, 77, 79, 82, 83, 84, 85, 86, 87, 95, 98, 107, 116, 121, 122, 129, 131
Reverbnation..99
RSS..71
Search engine optimization....................23, 25, 27, 33, 38
SEO...23, 25, 27, 29, 33
Social-bookmarking..125
Stream..55, 105, 106, 111
StumbleUpon......17, 18, 123, 125, 126, 127, 128, 129, 131, 132
Su.pr..58, 131, 132
Terms of Service...74, 76
Thumbs-Up...116, 127, 128
Traffic. .18, 22, 23, 31, 80, 81, 115, 116, 125, 127, 128, 131, 139
Tweet.......................49, 55, 56, 57, 59, 60, 65, 66, 67, 90, 105
Tweets.............................49, 55, 57, 59, 60, 65, 66, 90
TweetSched..60
Twitter. .16, 17, 18, 38, 41, 43, 46, 47, 49, 50, 51, 53, 54, 55, 56,

57, 58, 59, 60, 63, 65, 66, 67, 73, 90, 97, 105, 106, 116, 128, 131
Unfollow 63
URL 30, 53, 86, 116, 131
Videos 49, 91, 111, 115, 116, 117
Wicz 22
World Wide Web 44, 109
Yahoo 29
YouTube 17, 113, 115, 116
@ 56, 59, 97, 98
+1 .... 38, 105, 111

About the Author

Ken Powers was born in Billings, Montana. He lived and attended school in the small farming community of Conrad, Montana and after obtaining degrees in Computer Science and Industrial and Management Engineering from Montana State University in 1992, pursued a career as a professional luthier for the Gibson/Flatiron Mandolin and Banjo Company. In 1998 he continued his musically-based career path by becoming the Chief Brass Musical Instrument Repair Technician for Music Centers, Inc. in Tacoma, Washington. In 2004, he began his creative journey as a self-taught watercolor artist. It is through the very successful online marketing of his watercolor artwork that he began to effectively utilize social-media as a promotional tool. He is currently living in Tacoma, Washington with his wife and two children.